Sebastian, Remember that life is not a race or competition, It is a journey, so enjoy all the special moments. All our love Gram & Bubba

Counting Our Way to Maine

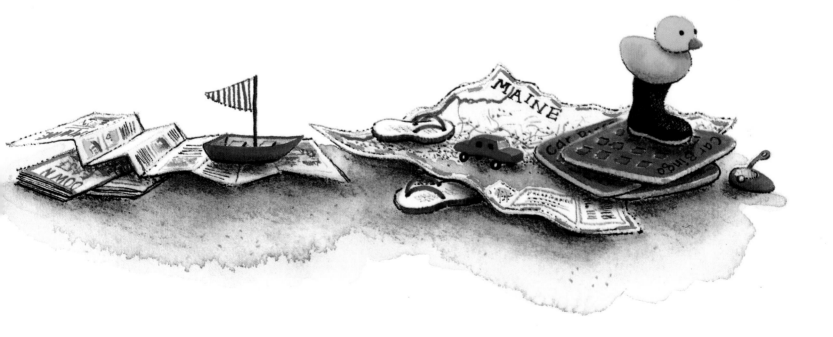

Printed in China February, 2014

ISBN: 978-0-89272-775-9

Down East Books
www.nbnbooks.com

Distributed to the trade by National Book Network, Inc.

Library of Congress Control Number: 2007943408

Counting Our Way to Maine

Maggie Smith

DownEastBooks

for Mom & Dad

1 For our trip to Maine this summer we packed one baby,

2 two dogs,

3 and three bicycles.

4 As we left the city behind us,
we passed four taxicabs

5 and five smokestacks.

6 We had to stop for the bathroom six times!

7 When we were halfway there, we stopped again and ate seven ice creams.

8 Then we climbed into the car and drove over and around eight mountains.

9 Before long we had to stop again.
Nine deer watched us.

10

When we finally arrived at the cottage, there were ten slugs waiting on the steps!

11

During our vacation, we built eleven sand castles.

12 We went down to the dock and saw twelve lobster pots

13 and thirteen boats.

14

As the fog lifted, we spotted fourteen buoys bobbing on the waves.

15

One hot day we climbed a steep hill and filled fifteen boxes with blueberries.

16 And the next day we made sixteen blueberry pies.

17 We went into the woods early one morning
and found seventeen mushrooms.

18

When we got back to the cottage, we counted eighteen mosquito bites!

19

For our cookout the last night we went to a nearby cove and dug nineteen clams.

20

That evening, as the tide crept in to say good-bye,

we chased twenty fireflies.

The next morning we let our fireflies go.

And for our trip back to the city
we packed one baby . . .